POETIC JOURNEY OF A JOYOUS OUTCOME

MARY MAGDALENE JOHNSON

Gotham Books

30 N Gould St.
Ste. 20820, Sheridan, WY 82801
https://gothambooksinc.com/

Phone: 1 (307) 464-7800

© 2023 *Mary M. Johnson*. All rights reserved.

No part of this book may be reproduced, stored in a retrieval system, or transmitted by any means without the written permission of the author.

Published by Gotham Books (June 8, 2023)

ISBN: 979-8-88775-319-5 (P)
ISBN: 979-8-88775-320-1 (E)

Because of the dynamic nature of the Internet, any web addresses or links contained in this book may have changed since publication and may no longer be valid.

The views expressed in this work are solely those of the author and do not necessarily reflect the views of the publisher, and the publisher hereby disclaims any responsibility for them.

TABLE OF CONTENTS

Introduction 1
"Judgment Being In The House Of God" 2
"Passion Of Christ" 3
"Jesus Has Loosing, For Your Life" 4
"Cross" 5
"Deep Waters Of Mine" 6
"Strife's And Conflicts" 7
"Valley Of Dry Bones" 8
"Comfort" 9
"Let Us Dwell In Him" 10
"Eye Hath Not Seen Nor Heard" 11
Vision 12
Signs And Wonders 13
My Yoke Is Easy My Burden Is Light 14
Peace Makers 15
Earthquake 16
Rejoice 17
Mercy 18
Heritage 19
Veil 20
Liars 21
The Scroll 22
Pot Of Honor 23
The Wrath Of God 24
Truth 25
Michael Arch Angel 26
Beatitudes Of Daily Living 27
Manifestation 28
Formulism 29
Pride 30
Precepts 31
Arise 32
Reflection 33

Success	34
Transitory	35
Eternal Tunnel Of Light	36
Kingdom Of Heaven	37
Everlasting Arms	38
Have Thy Way God	39
The Defilement Of The Holy Temple	40
A Heart Of Pearls	41
Peace That Surpasses Understanding	42
Love	43
Goodness Of God	44
Apprehensions	45
Time at Hand	46
Suffering Of Christians	47
Judging Is Within The Lord Our Savior	48
Antichrist	49
The Rapture	50
The Heavenly Wedding	51
Of An	54
Poetic Journey of an Joyous Outcome	55

Introduction

"Poetic Journey of a Joyous Outcome"

*An inner journey of inner stillness
that calls forth creation of life.
It is being made in the likeness of His image.
Sharing life, loving others and being
doers of the word.
The best is yet to come.
Being true worshippers;
put away the idols.
Like using shape, objects,
and golden calf dragon, etc;
Passion of Christ shared all things
to those who are strong
and endure to the end.
Being righteousness to God is
his Heritage of our birth right.*

BY: MARY M. JOHNSON

"Judgment Being In The House Of God"

Israel had become ripe in her sin and the end is here. Destruction has fallen upon the nation ready for judgment being in the house of God with business and material things on your mind and not spiritual things. In daily occupational demanding higher prices than being fair to the people forsaken the poor and needy. God will send a famine upon the land weeping sorrow and grief, dead bodies, not hungry for bread, not thirsts for water. People will be thirsty for the word of God, "ignored to hear," times is here. Upon Judgment Day!

BY: MARY M. JOHNSON

Many seek the ruler's favor; but every man's judgment cometh from the Lord.
PROV. 29:26 (KJV)

Many crave & seek the ruler's favor, but the wise man (waits) for justice from the Lord.
PROV. 29:26 (AMP)

"Passion Of Christ"

Changing the truth of God in a lie, "in place of true worship"
then placing idols in his place.
He left them and let them do the shameful things.
Men and Women have done.
Things of their bodies receive punishment for their wrong.
My good servant will make people right with God.
He'll share all things to these who are strong.
True Christian for the Passion of Christ
shall endure to the end of time for they know not what they do.

BY: MARY M. JOHNSON

But ye are in the flesh but in the Spirit if so be that the Spirit of God dwell in you. Now if any man have not the Spirit of Christ he is none of his.

ROM. 9:9 (KJV)

But you are not living the life of the flesh, you are living the life of the Spirit, if the (Holy) Spirit of God (really) dwells within you (directs & controls you). But if anyone does not possess the (Holy) Spirit of Christ, he is none of His (he does not belong to Christ, is not truly a child of God)

ROM. 9:9 (AMP)

"Jesus Has Loosing, For Your Life"

Whether it's a spirit of infirmity that weakens your body;
he has loosing for your life of eternity.
Whether it's a spirit of legalism that's got a hold of your soul;
he has a loosing for you to gain.
Spiritualism, let go of Criticism,
whether it's doubt or fear or your own pride.
He has a loosing for you to stride
within yourself loose him and let go.
Lo, I am with you always, and to the end.

BY: MARY M. JOHNSON

For what is a man profited, if he shall gain the whole world, and lose his own soul? or what shall a man give in exchange for his soul?

MAT. 16:26 (KJV)

For what will it profit a man if he gain the whole world and forfeits his life (his blessed life in the kingdom of God)? Or what would a man give as an exchange foe his (blessed) life (in the kingdom of God)?

MAT. 16:26 (AMP)

"Cross"

Through the cross of Jesus, my world was crucified;
the thing is being the new people God made.
If people want to follow me,
they must be willing to give up their daily lives to follow me.
Those who give up their lives for me have true life
on the cross so that our sinful selves
would have no power over us and we would be slaves to sin.
God made you alive with Christ to forgive our sins,
he cancel all the debt listed
all the record with its rule fail and nail it to the cross.

BY: MARY M. JOHNSON

And he that taketh not his cross, and followeth after me, is not worthy of me.

MAT. 10:38(KJV)

And he who does not take up his cross and follow Me (cleave steadfastly to Me, conforming wholly to My example in living and, if need be, in dying also) is not worthy of Me.

MAT. 10:38(AMP)

"Deep Waters Of Mine"

Lord lift me up, the waters are up to my neck, I am far from the deck. The smile on my face is drying and I am weary with my crying. My eyes waste They rejoice at me staying that way, I know it's a bright day. Lord you know my sins, Lord you know my friends. There is none like you that will pull me through. My enemies look at me with hate while thy judge within the gate. Lord you cause the winds to blow and the flood waters to overflow. They appear before me with sign, hoping that I'll go under, while they plunder the harbor. Let your salvation, O God set me upon high I will magnify you with thanksgiving, in the land of the living and the giving.

BY: MARY M. JOHNSON

When the poor & needy seek water, & there is none, & their tongue faileth for thirst, I the Lord will hear them, I the God of Israel will not forsake them.

IS. 41:17 (KJV)

The poor & needy are seeking water there is none; their tongues are parched with thirst, I the Lord will answer them; I, the God of Israel will not forsake them.

IS. 41:17 (AMP)

"Strife's And Conflicts"

*Hatred stir up trouble, love forgives all wrong;
don't move old stones that mark a border. Love your
neighbors as you love yourself. Don't take fields that belongs to the
fatherless that don't tell their values, items, and homes that
set up for them. Kind words from a wicked mind tell a shining,
a coat on a clay pot. The Lord hates sacrifices offered by the wicked, it
better to eat dry crust of bread in peace than to feast in quarrelling a quick
temper and sins a lot. Stick with love for angry and fighting over words it
brings jealousy soaking against evil mistrust.*

BY: MARY M. JOHNSON

Hatred stirreth up strife's: but love covereth all sins.

PROV. 10:12 (KJV)

Hatred stirs up contentions, but love covers all transgressions.

PROV. 10:12 (AMP)

"Valley Of Dry Bones"

*In the valley of guilt, sorrow and broken hearts
ruin cities as well as
nations surrounded in darkness,
deserted and destroyed
habitations.
Dreams and hopes gone being
disobedient to his command these
bones are house of Israel the
Lord spoke to Ezekiel.
Prophecy to the bones that the
promise of life you breathe into
them, you take it away by you
they exist you make the land new again,
stop doing evil.*

BY: MARY M. JOHNSON

1 The hand of the Lord was upon me, and carried me out in the spirit of the Lord, and set me down in the midst of the valley which *was* full *of* bones 2 And caused me to pass by them round about and behold *there were* very many in the open valley; and lo, *they were* very dry. 3 and he said unto me, Son of man, can these bones live? And I answered, O Lord God, thou knowest. 4 Again he said unto me, Prophesy upon these bones, and say unto them, O ye dry bones, hear the word of the Lord. 5 Thus saith the Lord God unto these bones; Behold, I *will* cause breath to enter into you, and ye shall live:

EZEK. 37:1-5 (KJV)

1 THE HAND of the Lord was upon me, and He brought me out in the spirit of the Lord and set me down in the midst of the valley; and it was full *of* bones 2 And He caused me to pass round about among them, an behold, *there were* very many [human bones] in the open valley or plain and behold, they were very dry. 3 And He said to me Son of man, cam these bones live? And I answered, O Lord God, You know! 4 Again He said to me, Prophesy to these bones, hear the word of the Lord. 5 Them says the Lord God to these bones; Behold I *will* cause breath and spirit to enter you, and you shall live:

EZEK. 37:1-5 (AMP)

"Comfort"

*Encourage each other through our prayers
and support making the more cheerful
giving hope and strength making trouble
easier to bear.*

*Comfort the feeble minded those of
little soul the faint hearted, those in
a battle let them do the best they can.*

*No man speaking by the spirit without
divine inspiration forgives him and
comfort him. You give me comfort in
all my troubles their great joy.*

BY: MARY M. JOHNSON

Now we exhort you, brethren warn them that are unruly, comfort the feebleminded, support the weak, be patient toward all men.

1 THES. 5:14 (KJV)

And we earnestly beseech you, brethren, admonish (warn and seriously advise) those who are out of line [the loafers, the disorderly, and the unruly]; encourage the timid and fainthearted, help and give your support to the weak soul, [and] be very patient with everybody [always keeping your temper].

1 THES. 5:14 (AMP)

"Let Us Dwell In Him"

Live in at night way like people belong to a day. No wild parties or get drunk, no sins of any kind and no fighting we belong to the day so we can control ourselves. We should wear faith and live to protect ourselves. We come before the throne where there grace. So we have grown up teaching be near God with a sincere heart. We hold firm of confessing and trusting God to do his promises.
Let us live and do good deeds that we run the race and never give up. Jesus suffered outside the city to make his people, with his own blood. Though Jesus we offer God sacrifice of praises from our lips.

BY: MARY M. JOHNSON

And what agreement hath the temple of God with idols? For ye are the temple of the living God; as God hath said, I will dwell in them, and walk in them; and I will be their God, and they shall be my people.

2 COR. 6:16(KJV)

What agreement [can there be between] a temple of God with idols? For we are the temple of the living God; even as God said, I will dwell in and with and among them; and I will be their God, and they shall be my people.

2 COR.6:16 (AMP)

"Eye Hath Not Seen Nor Heard"

*Man knows not the divine plan for
him, only by the increase he
posses no one knows the
treasures stirred within him.*

*No man can define what good is.
God's grace is sufficient in all
things turn within the silence
in the stillness of his peace.*

*Bless are the ears for they to hear.
Fear of God is the
beginning of all wisdom.*

BY: MARY M. JOHNSON

Then saith he to Thomas, Reach hither thy finger, and behold my hands; and reach hither thy hand, and thrust it into my side: and be not faithless, but believing.

ST. JOHN 20:27 (KJV)

Then He said to Thomas, Reach out your finger here, and see My hands; and out your hand and place [it] in My side. Do not be faithless and incredulous, but [stop your unbelief and believe!

ST. JOHN 20:27 (AMP)

Vision

*Where there is no vision the people perish;
as problem arise that can't be solved,
unless we have the vision of power
within which is greater than ungodly things.*

*The old ideas of man are weak and
ungodly; new vision is truth of
our being be holding new
strength in our busy lives
and relationship with others.*

*They are worthy, Oh Lord to
receive glory, honor and
power all creation
acknowledge supreme power
of God.*

*He made all things for his
pleasure and same way he protects us.*

BY: MARY M. JOHNSON

Where there is no vision, the people perish: but he that keepeth the law, happy is he.

PROV. 29:18 (KJV)

Where there is no vision [no redemptive revelation of God], the people perish: but he who keeps the law [of God which includes that of man]- blessed (happy, fortunate, and enviable) is he.

PROV. 29:18 (AMP)

<u>Signs And Wonders</u>

*Your praises from where the sunrises and to where it set;
when the people cry for help he will send
someone to save and defend them.
God approve by using wonders great signs many kinds of miracles and
by giving people gifts through the Holy Spirit.*

*God's deeds are inspiring and righteousness
even to men at the end of the earth.
God's grace is a wonder beyond human understanding, love is so
amazing, so I've demand my soul, my life, my all,
I stand all amaze at the love Jesus offers me
the world is full of wonders.*

BY: MARY M. JOHNSON

Then said Jesus unto him, Except ye see signs and wonders, ye will not believe.

ST. JOHN 4:48 (KJV)

Then Jesus said to him, Unless you see signs and miracles happen, you [people] never will believe (trust, have faith) at all.

ST. JOHN 4:48 (AMP)

My Yoke Is Easy My Burden Is Light

We use higher state of Christ hood, when we give up selfishness desires, wants, and wishes.

The burden is great when we carry it ourselves.

When we know there is a shoulder to carry our burdens on.

Come unto me all ye that labor and are heavy laden, I will give you rest.

We shall find rest in unto yourselves; yes you can rest your burdens on my shoulder.

Christ makes itself endurance in your life will be less of you carry the burden.

BY: MARY M. JOHNSON

Then Jesus said, "Come to me, all of you who are weary and carry heavy burdens, and I will give you rest. Take my yoke upon you. Let me teach you, because I am humble and gentle, and you will find rest for your souls. For my yoke fits perfectly, and the burden I give you is light." Mat.

11:28-30 (KJV)

Then Jesus said, "Come to Me, all you who labor and are heavy-laden and overburdened, and I will cause you rest [I will ease and relieve and refresh your souls]. Take My yoke upon you and learn of Me, for I am gentle (meek) and humble (lowly) in heart, and you will find rest (relief and ease and refreshment and recreation and blessed quiet) for your souls. For My yoke is wholesome (useful, good-not harsh, hard sharp, or pressing, but comfortable, gracious, and pleasant), and My burden is light and easy to be borne.

MAT. 11:28-30 (AMP)

Peace Makers

*All things of God-all wise and mighty being total
change of heart, soul and life takes place
under preaching the Gospel power and grace
of God, A change of heart disposal to accept salvation.*

*Peace makers labor for the good instead of fanning
the fire of strife. Be one mind in unity, be friendly
minded, and not render evil for evil your business to do well.*

*To implore God blessing on your worst enemy, walk in
righteousness live in place. The eye of God is over
the righteous and his ears to their prayers.*

BY: MARY M. JOHNSON

But the wisdom that is from above is first pure, then peaceable, gentle and easy to be in-treated, full of mercy and good fruits, without partiality, and without hypocrisy.

JAS. 3:17(KJV)

But the wisdom from heaven is first of all pure (undefiled); then it is also peace-loving, courteous (considerate, gentle) [It is willing to] yield to reason, full compassion and good fruits; it is wholehearted and straightforward, impartial and unfeigned (free from doubts, wavering and insincerity).

JAS. 3:17(KJV)

Earthquake

A thick cloud where God peaks out of darkness to sanctify, Let them wash their clothes in his presence.
Everything is clean and pure Thou shut its bounds; the place is sacred because God is a consuming fire that's a fearful thing to fall in the hands of the living God. He reigns in the heart of man that believes; His kingdom peace joy and the Holy Spirit. Let us have grace hold fast to the kingdom.
In a little while I'll shake the nation; Desire of all nation come that the house be full with glory.

BY: MARY M. JOHNSON

And the Lord said unto Satan, Hast thou considered my servant Job, that there is none like him in the earth, a perfect and an upright man, one that feareth God, and escheweth evil? And still he holdeth fast his integrity, although thou movedst me against him, to destroy him without cause.

JOB 2:1 (KJV)

And the Lord said unto Satan, Have you considered My servant Job, that there is none like him on the earth, a blameless and upright man, one who [reverently] fears God, and abstains from and shuns all evil [because it is wrong]? And still he holds fast his integrity, although you moved Me against him to destroy him without cause.

JOB 2:1 (AMP)

Rejoice

*The Lord God is king, you are
my help because of your protection
I sing. Our ancestors turn against
your kindness of the Dead Sea
we were given power greater
than the enemy. You shouldn't be
happy because the spirit obeys
you; your name was written
in heaven the same is joy in
presence of angels of God, when
a sinner changes his heart and life.*

*Be happy you are sharing Christ
suffering; you'll be full of joy
when he comes again in glory.*

BY: MARY M. JOHNSON

Who now rejoice in sufferings for you, and fill up that which is behind of the afflictions of Christ in my flesh for his body's sake, which is the church.

COL. 1:24(KJV)

[Even] now I rejoice in the midst of my sufferings on your behalf. And in my own person I am making up whatever is still lacking and remains to be completed [on our part fill up that which is behind of the afflictions of Christ in my flesh for his body's sake, which is the church.

COL. 1:24(AMP)

<u>*Mercy*</u>

*His mercy is great and he loves so much, those who show
mercy to others are happy; because God show mercy to them,
so you must show mercy, Mercy can stand without fear.*

*He won't leave you or destroy nor forget the agreement
of your ancestor when he swore to them I am the Lord who shows
mercy and kindness who doesn't angry quickly.*

*He cause us to be born again in living hope, he saves through
the cleansing of his blood that made us new through the holy spirit.*

BY: MARY M. JOHNSON

The Lord is merciful and gracious, slow to anger, and plenteous in mercy.

PS 103:8 (KJV)

The Lord is merciful and gracious, slow to anger and plenteous in mercy and loving-kindness.

PS 103:8 (AMP)

Heritage

*If the Lord doesn't build their house
the builders are working for nothing
I will give them a long life they see
how I can save.*

*When people are tempted strong
And proven their faith,
God promise those who love him
a new heaven and earth where
goodness lives; through this, he
gives great and precious things.*

*These gifts you share being like
God so the gift won't ruin
you with evil desires.*

*God choose the poor to be rich in faith to become the kingdom,
God promise those who love him,
so with Jesus he'll give you all things.*

BY: MARY M. JOHNSON

No weapon that is formed against thee shall prosper; and every tongue that shall rise against thee in judgments thou shalt condemn. This is the heritage of the servants of the Lord, and their righteousness is of me, saith the Lord.

IS. 54:17 (KJV)

But no weapon that is formed against you shall prosper, and every tongue that shall rise against you in judgments you shall show to be in the wrong. This [peace, righteousness, security, triumph over opposition] is the heritage of the servants of the Lord [those in whom the ideal Servant of the Lord is reproduced]; this is the righteousness or the vindication which they obtain form Me [this is that which I impart to them as their justification], days the Lord.

IS. 54:17 (AMP)

Veil

*The Kingdom of heaven is open to all believers
let us draw near with blood to the throne of God with a true heart
deeply convince of our heart and help in earnest in full assurance of faith.*

*Trust God we are free to enter the most high place with out fear.
We can enter through the curtain Christ body.
We can draw nigh to good,
from a full evil mind.
Peace and love of God shed abroad in our hearts by the Holy Ghost.*

BY: MARY M. JOHNSON

Which hope we have as an anchor of the soul both sure and steadfast, and which enterth into that within the veil.

HEB. 6:19 (KJV)

[Now] we have this [hope] as a sure and steadfast anchor of the soul [it cannot slip and it cannot break sown under whoever steps out upon it-a hope] that reaches farther and enters into [the very certainty of the Presence] within the veil

HEB. 6:19 (AMP)

Liars

*Ye are your father the devil you are the seed of the old serpent my word
has no place for you; you hear
the truth of God but don't heed the
word of life, has no place in you.*

*The wickedest ranged from the
womb which decree of God
as a melted snail that smears
the track, which don't see the sun.*

*Though I redeemed them of my
love and power; we are one
body in Christ and he's the
head as a man right hand
wouldn't deceive or wrong
his left hand. Deal honest
with each other Lord save me from liars and those which plan evil.*

BY: MARY M. JOHNSON

God forbid: yea, let God be true, but every man a liar; as it is written,
That thou mightiest be justified in thy saying, and mightiest overcome
when thou art judged.

ROM.3:4 (KJV)

By no means! Let God be found true though every human being is false and
a liar, as it is written, That You may be justified and shown to be upright
in what You say, and prevail when You are judged [by sinful men].

ROM. 3:4 (AMP)

The Scroll

All the host of heaven shall be dissolved roll up like a scroll. Their host shall fall down as the leaf falls from the vine and fruit falling from the tree. The sky receded as a scroll when it rolled up every mountain and island will move out of its place.

Then I said behold I came in the scroll of the book it's written of me.

BY: MARY M. JOHNSON

This shall be written for the generation to come: and the people which shall be created shall praise the Lord.

PS.103:18 (KJV)

Let this be recorded for the generation yet unborn, that a people yet to be created shall praise the Lord.

PS.103:18 (AMP)

Pot Of Honor

*Does not the potter have power over
the clay from the same lump makes
one vessel for honor and another for
dishonor? What if God wants to show
anger and make his power known?
We know all things work for the good
of those who love him.
Not in passion of lust, like those
who do not know God, no one
shall defraud his brother in this matter.
The Lord is the quencher of such if any
one cleanses him self from the latter.
He is vessel for honor excellences
power of God not us.*

BY: MARY M. JOHNSON

Hath not the potter power over they clay, of the same lump to make one vessel unto honour, and another unto dishonor?

ROM.9:21 (KJV)

Has the potter no right over the clay, to make out of the same mass (lump) one vessel for beauty and distinction and honorable use, and another for menial or ignoble and dishonorable use?

ROM.9:21 (AMP)

The Wrath Of God

*All our days pass with an angry; our years end with Amazon.
We know that everything God made has been waiting until
new in pain like a woman ready to give birth.
God shows his anger through his knowledge being
made clean to them. Being stubborn and refusing to
change makes your own punishment, not being able to
obtain the knowledge of truth; on that day every one sees
God's righteous judgment. Live for God glory and honor
for life has no end, God gives forgivers love. He gives trouble
and suffering to those who does evil, that worship the beast
evil ideals taking the mark on the forehead in hand will also
drink the wine of God anger being in pain and suffering
will bring sculpture before the holy angel and the lamb.*

BY: MARY M. JOHNSON

But the Lord is true God; he is the living God and an everlasting king: at his wrath the earth shall tremble, and the nations shall not be able to abide his indignation.

JER. 10:10 (KJV)

But the Lord is the true God and the God of truth (the God Who is Truth). He is the living He is the living God and the everlasting King. At His Wrath the earth quakes, and the nations are not able to bear His indignations

JER. 10:10 (AMP)

Truth

*I am the way that leads to the father;
the truth that teaches knowledge
of God and direction to those
who seek and serve.
The spirits of truth to
Manifest apply the
truth, desires the flesh.*

*The eyes of pride of life
cannot reserve the spirit
of truth. Dedicate
consecrated to the
Ministry separated
from worldly concerns.
Christ is the law of
justification to uprightly
standing; setting good
honest righteous.*

BY: MARY M. JOHNSON

Jesus saith unto him, I am the way, the truth, and the life: no man cometh unto the Father but by me.

JOHN 14:6 (KJV)

Jesus said to him, I am the Way and the Truth and the Life; no one comes to the Father except by (through) me.

JOHN 14:6 (AMP)

Michael Arch Angel

*Michael who led the loyal angels in defeating
Satan the dragon and his angels lost their place in heaven;
home of God. He was thrown down from heaven the
old snake Satan who tricks the whole world.
Jesus gone into heaven at God's right hand side ruling
over angels' authority and power. Those who worship
idols should be ashamed let all God angels worship him.
The angels became his wind; his servant; the flame of
fire his presence and power. All his angels are spirits who
serve him are sent to help those who'll receive salvation be
joyful, prayerful and give thanks in whatever happens
this is what god wants for you in Christ.*

BY: MARY M. JOHNSON

In all their affliction he was afflicted, and the angel of his presence saved them: in his love and in his pity he redeemed them; and he bare them, and carried them all the days of old.

IS.63:9 (KJV)

In all their affliction He was afflicted, and the Angel of His presence saved them; in His love and His pity He redeemed them; and He lifted them up and carried them all the days old.

IS.63:9 (AMP)

Beatitudes Of Daily Living

Let not your heart be troubled by accusations of others.
Bless one another; Jesus knew their minds
as he spoke to the man with the withered hand
it's restored and wholeness as the other.
You should love your God with all your heart,
mind, and soul don't be sad rejoice and be exceedingly glad.
Bless and press toward the mark of great reward in heaven.

BY: MARY M. JOHNSON

Let not your heart be troubled: ye believe in God, believe also in me.
JOHN 14:1 (KJV)

Do Not let your hearts be troubled (distressed, agitated). You believe in and adhere to and trust in and rely also on Me.
JOHN 14:1 (AMP)

Manifestation

What known of God is made clear of them? Christ himself which is in you; thanks be to God who led us to victory through Christ.

God uses us to spread knowledge everywhere like a sweet perfume to those who are saved; we are the smell of life.

Then life brings life, these who follow the truth that comes to the light it shows the things done through God

BY: MARY M. JOHNSON

Therefore judge nothing before the time until the Lord come, who both will bring to light the hidden things of darkness, and will make manifest the counsels of the hearts: and then shall every man have praise of God.

1 COR. 4:5 (KJV)

So do not make any hasty or premature judgments before the time when the Lord comes [again], for He will both bring to light the secret things that are [now hidden] in darkness and disclose and expose the [secret] aims (motives and purpose) of hearts. Then ever man will receive his [due] commendation from God.

1 COR. 4:5 (AMP)

Formulism

*You are lukewarm neither hot or cold has you become wealthy
not needing anything you'll blind to your own shame.
Do you see people skilled in their work; they will work for Kings
not for ordinary people. In the last days people trust themselves
they say evil things against their friends they go in homes of
women in their sin led by evil desires advises you to buy gold.
Underneath your soul is truly rich,
peace to those who depend upon him because they trust in him.*

BY: MARY M. JOHNSON

Because thou sayest, I am rich, and increased with goods, and have need of nothing; and knowest not that thou art wretched, and miserable, and poor, and blind, and naked:

REV. 3:17 (KJV)

For you say, I am rich; I have prospered and grown wealthy, and I am in need of nothing; and you do not realize and understand that you are wretched, pitiable, poor, blind, and naked

REV. 3:17 (AMP)

Pride

*For all that is in the world all that
can boast of all it compromise is
only sensitive. Neither attack
comes, from nor lead to, God "they are the world".
Deprive the mind from divine
wisdom be hold his soul, which is
lifted up he that presumes on his
safety without any special warning from God.*

*God is a proud man which he
confesses or thinks of him. To
live eternal by grace of God
believes in Christ will posses their souls in quietness and confidence*

BY: MARY M. JOHNSON

Pride goeth before destruction and a haughty spirit before a fall.

PRO. 16:18 (KJV)

Pride goes before destruction and a haughty spirit before a fall.

PRO. 16:18 (AMP)

Precepts

This is what I'll do,
"You'll my sure in life, I pray to you with all my heart,
and have mercy on me as you promise".
I thought of my life looking unto you in the middle of the night.
I get up to thank you, and your love is right.
Teaching me and trusting in your commands,
calling forth wisdom and knowledge.
Your hands made me and the earth as it still stands.
I lean not on my own understanding;
As God is in control and He orders my steps.

BY: MARY M. JOHNSON

I will meditate in thy precepts, and have respect unto thy ways.

PS. 119:15 (KJV)

I will meditate on Your precepts and have respect to Your ways [the paths of life marked out by Your law].

PS 119:15 (AMP)

Arise

The sun raises, the sun sets and hurries back where it rises again. Arise and shine to the countenance f his time. The glory of the Lord shines on you, nations will come to your light. Kings will come to the brightness if your sun rises. Some like seeds planted on a stalled ground, hears the word and accepts it with joy. Some like seeds planted on rocky ground, instead don't allow the word to go deep for only a short time. Persecution and trouble blocks the flow of growth like a thorny weed. Clear and clean your mind, so you can bear good fruits in your daily life and glow for His kingdom.

BY: MARY M. JOHNSON

But for you that fear my name shall the Sun of righteousness arise with healing in his wings; and ye shall go forth and grow up as calves of the stall.

MAL. 4:2 (KJV)

But unto you who revere and worshipfully fear My name shall the Sun of Righteousness arise with healing in His wings and his beams, and you shall go forth and gambol like calves [released] from the stall and leap for joy.

MAL 4:2 (AMP)

Reflection

*Nothing can replace the wise decisions
God helps me to make.
A sound decision whether you turn
right or left your ear will hear a
voice saying this is the days walk.
Humble yourself before you fall,
repent soon as sin is committed
and let nothing prevent you
from making a vow in good times.
The wise be caution in everything
in sinful times, take care not
to offend every person of sense,
recognize wisdom and will respect
anyone who found her.*

BY: MARY M. JOHNSON

If you people, which are called by my name, shall humble themselves, and pray, and seek my face, and turn from their wicked ways; then will I hear from heaven, and will forgive their sin, and will heal their land. 2

CHR. 7:14 (KJV)

If My people, who are called by My name, shall humble themselves, pray seek, crave, and require of necessity My face and turn form their wicked ways, then will I hear from heaven, for give their sin, and heal their land.

2 CHR. 7:14 (AMP)

Success

Success falls on my nest when I do my best;
life is full of surprises I'm ready when he arise.
I'm always giving toward the living;
I don't rely on others, not either my brothers;
I'll keep growing my business.
When I'm under stress I let God do the rest.
I stick with my books and stay away from crooks,
I make contact with facts.
I stay away from fiction that will leave me
in an awful position.

Success is a way to be blessed, and lead to
happiness. I don't deprive, I always strive.

BY: MARY M. JOHNSON

Not that we are sufficient of ourselves to think anything as of ourselves;
but our sufficiency is of God.

2 COR. 3:5 (KJV)

It is not that we think we can do anything of lasting value by ourselves.
Our only power and success come from God.

2 COR. 3:5 (AMP)

Transitory

*My day is a hand breath; my life all time swallowed up in eternity, every man at his best and exists in vanity. A thousand years a day in thy sight, a day passes like a watch in the night falling asleep.
All our days pass under your wrath, our lives over like a sigh. Acquaint ourselves with thee being at peace.
We may die in thy favor live and reign with thee in eternal.
Love not the world begins flourish and end depriving the mind of spiritual enjoyment.*

BY: MARY M. JOHNSON

And it is easier for heaven and earth to pass, than one title of the law to fail.

LUKE 16:17 (KJV)

Yet it is easier for heaven and earth to pass away than for one dot of the Law to fail and become void.

LUKE 16:17 (AMP)

Eternal Tunnel Of Light

Satan's power surrounded with schemes and lies.
God rules the land your power is greater than man.
Love, grace, faith and prayer are the keys To Your Kingdom.
In you we move and have our being, I'm overcoming my past tenses
and coming to my senses. Lord, "let your light shine through me and
nurture my soul with harmony and severity and calamity.
You say in your word:
Lean on the Everlasting Light, We Walk by Faith and Not by Sight.

BY: MARY M. JOHNSON

The eternal God is thy refuge, and underneath are the everlasting arms:
and he shall thrust out the enemy from; and shall say, Destroy them.

DEUT. 33:27 (KJV)

The eternal God is your refuge and dwelling place, and underneath are the everlasting
arms' He drove the enemy before you and thrust them out saying, Destroy!

DEUT. 33:27 (AMP)

Kingdom Of Heaven

Nation against nation, kingdom against kingdom, the Lord does things right and true, everyone will respect you. He opens up the gates, good people will enter, living right with peace and joy in the Holy Spirit the good seed belong to his children of his kingdom. The weeds are those people belong to the evil one harvest time at the end of the world the son of man will send his angels those who do sin and evil will be thrown in the furnace. Crying and gridding in pain the good people shine like the sun in the kingdom of the father.

BY: MARY M. JOHNSON

And saying, Repent ye: for the kingdom of heaven is at hand.

MATT. 3:2 (KJV)

And saying repent (think differently; change you mind, regretting your sins and changing your conduct), for the kingdom of heaven is at hand.

MATT. 3:2 (AMP)

Everlasting Arms

*Lord all powerful who is
like you, you scatter your
enemies, you power earth
and skies belong to you.
You made the world of
everything in your creation
joy is in your name! Your
right hand lifted us up love
and truth you do.
You're right holy arm win
the victory power and
strength. He is coming to
rule the people for their
obedient trusting him.*

BY: MARY M. JOHNSON

The eternal God is thy refuge, and underneath are the everlasting arms: and he shall thrust out the enemy from before thee; and shall say, Destroy them.

DEUT. 33:27 (KJV)

The eternal God is your refuge and dwelling place, and underneath are the everlasting arms; He drove the enemy before you and thrust them out saying, Destroy!

DEUT. 33:27 (AMP)

<u>*Have Thy Way God*</u>

For the ways of the Lord is right, Just and true are his ways who is wise let him understand, who is discreet; let him know them.

Acknowledge him in all his ways his word must be entertained over and over through out the day and night for his help is at hand

BY: MARY M. JOHNSON

In all thy ways acknowledge him, and he shall direct thy paths.

PROV. 3:6 (KJV)

In all your ways know, recognize. And acknowledge Him, and He will direct and make straight and plain your paths.

PROV. 3:6 (AMP)

The Defilement Of The Holy Temple

*The heathen come into thy holy temple; they set fire to your
sanctuary and have no desire to serve you
They saith in their hearts, let us destroy them together,
they destroyed the meeting places in the land.*

*O God, how long? Will they blaspheme your name forever?
Why do you withdraw your hand even your right hand?
For you O God is working salvation in the midst of the earth,
the day and night is yours! You prepared the light and sun;
foolish people have blasphemed your name.
The dark places of the earth are full of the cruelty.*

*Don't let the oppressed return ashamed,
let the poor and needy praise your name.*

BY: MARY M. JOHNSON

If any man defile the temple of God, and that the Spirit of God dwelleth in you?

1 COR. 3:17 (KJV)

If anyone does hurt to God's temple or corrupts it [with false doctrines] or destroys it, God will do hurt to him and bring him to the corruption of death and destroy him. For the temple of God is holy (sacred to Him) and that [temple] you [the believing church and its individual believers] are.

1 COR. 3:17 (AMP)

A Heart Of Pearls

Having a heart to do as the Lord commands
and with stand among trail times. A pearl of
pure, faith, and trust knowing as one with
God. Being obedience of God, traveling
these pools watching and
caring for our souls. A
pearl of true divine,
can't be bought with
natural hands, pulling
hurt feelings of
resentment aside; a heart
of forgiving love, trusting
God spirit within us.
These pearls lay upon him
flowing and glowing preparing
people for works and service by
finding them a place in Christ.
Bring forth good in all concerns.

BY: MARY M. JOHNSON

A new heart also will I give you, and a new spirit will I put within you:
and I will take away the stony heart out of your flesh, and ii will give you
a heat of flesh.

EZEK. 36:26 (KJV)

A new heart will I give you and a new spirit will I put within you, and I
will take away the stony heart out of your flesh and give you a heart of
flesh.

EZEK 36:26 (AMP)

Peace That Surpasses Understanding

God is the center of command and the prince of peace.
God is not the author confusion and illusion.
"Peace is the gift of God!"
He who lifts our soul from outer forces,
Leads us into the inner sounds of joy.
Peace of God which surpassed all understanding.
Shall keep your heart, and mind through Jesus Christ.

BY: MARY M. JOHNSON

So that thou incline thine ear unto wisdom, and apply thine heart to understanding;

PROV. 2:2 (KJV)

Making your ear attentive to skilled and godly Wisdom and inclining and directing your heart and mind to understanding [applying all your powers to the quest for it]:

PROV. 2:2 (AMP)

Love

*Love cast out fear and it's so
near that he values me with a
love pure and constant as I
am right here and now.
God loves me in those
moments, when I'm act my
best and at my worst.
His love blesses with self
confident to value who I am
and the ability to express Love.
Love is patient, kind, it
bears all things we cast our
care on him and love never ends*

BY: MARY M. JOHNSON

There is no fear in love; but perfect love casteth out fear; because fear hath torment. He that fearth is not made perfect in love.

1 JOHN 4:18 (KJV)

There is no fear in love [dread does not exist], but full-grown (complete, perfect) love turns fear out of doors and expels every trace of terror! For fear brings with it the thought of punishment and [so] he who is afraid has not reached the full maturity of love [is not yet grown into love's complete perfection).

1 JOHN 4:18 (AMP)

Goodness Of God

Proud why do you brag about the evil you do?
God love is forever.

Happy are the people you choose, and
invite to stay in your court.

We are filled with good things in
your temple; all day long they
twisted my words.

Their plan are against me,
He is good to everyone he made to
enjoy the fruits of life.

BY: MARY M. JOHNSON

I had fainted, unless I had believed to see the goodness of the Lord in the land of the living.

PS. 27:13 (KJV)

[What would have become of me] had I not believed that I would see the Lord's goodness in the land of the living!

PS. 27:13 (AMP)

Apprehensions

Can you understand the search of God?
Can you search the limits of the Almighty?
His limits are higher in Heaven.
You cannot reach his limit,
who has the mind of the Lord, he will teach them.
For the mind of these people is stubborn.
They can't hear with their ears and close their eyes.
They will not understand what they see with their eyes.

Only the Apprehensions might understand in their minds.
Come to me, those who will not preach the good news.
With the help of the Holy Spirit,
Who will send from heaven thing into which is a desire to look.

BY: MARY M. JOHNSON

Trust in the Lord with all thine heart; and lean not unto thine own understanding.

PROV. 3:5 (KJV)

Lean on Trust in and be confident in the Lord with all your heart and mind and so not rely on your own insight or understanding.

PROV. 3:5 (AMP)

Time at Hand

*The spiritual city has real
foundation planned and built by God.
The way people understand slowness
God is able to do for you he plans
time and action for all things
he judges good and bad.*

*A Time for love and peace and to hate
war, why don't I let my self enjoy life.
This is sad and useless are you ready
today for me before the rooster
crows you say three times.*

*I don't know go clear your mind,
neither do the angels only the father
always be ready you don't
know when and where.*

BY: MARY M. JOHNSON

Blessed is he that considereth the poor: the Lord will deliver him in time of trouble

PS. 41:1 (KJV)

Blessed (Happy, fortunate to be envied) is he who considers the weak and the poor; the Lord will. deliver him in the time of evil and trouble.

PS. 41:1 (AMP)

Suffering Of Christians

*Being insulted because you
follow Christ you are blessed
for the spirit of the glory of
God rest upon you.
Suffering as God
wants, should trust their souls
to the water as they
do what is right.
For Christ suffer once for sins.
The just for the unjust that
he might bring us to God
being put to death in the flesh
but made alive by the spirit
Be happy that you
share Christ suffering and
cares for one another, be
secure and watch in your prayer.*

BY: MARY M. JOHNSON

But rejoice, inasmuch as ye are partakers of Christ's sufferings; that when his glory shall be revealed, ye may be glad also with exceeding joy.

1 PETER 4:13 (KJV)

But insofar as you are sharing Christ's sufferings, rejoice, so that when His glory [full of radiance and splendor] is revealed, you may also rejoice with triumph [exultantly].

1 PETER 4:13 (AMP)

Judging Is Within The Lord Our Savior

The rising of the sun and it's going down;
he is always there in despair.
Let the heaven declare his righteousness, God himself is judge.

Let not your heart withhold grudges of one another offer to
God thanksgiving and say your vows to the most high.
Call upon me in the day of trouble, He'll deliver you and
you shall glorify his name, I am God your God.

You spoke wicked things against others, whoever offers praises, glorify
me and to him who orders his conduct alright.
Be wises, I will show the salvation of God.

BY: MARY M. JOHNSON

For the Lord is our judge, the Lord is our lawgiver, the Lord is our king; he will save us.

IS.33:22 (KJV)

For the Lord is our Judge, the Lord is our Lawgiver, the4 Lord is our King; He will save us.

IS. 33:22 (AMP)

Antichrist

Who is the liar, the person who doesn't accept Jesus as his Lord and savior! Who appears and exalts himself alone godly worship setting in the holy temple taking the highest place belongs to the most high.
Satan sends his signs lying wonders and miracles, who deny Jesus in flesh. Who God shall consume blasting him that he wither and die away, by the spirit of his mouth words of eternal life true destroys man of his sin.
God sends his messiah with real miracles signs and wonders. This is the last of grace and mercy to mankind any body opposes to Jesus and spread of his gospel is antichrist.

BY: MARY M. JOHNSON

For Many deceivers are entered into the world, who confess not that Jesus Christ is come in the flesh. This is a deceiver and an antichrist.

2 JOHN 1:7 (KJV)

For many imposters (seducers, deceivers, and false leaders) have gone out into the world, men who will not acknowledge (confess, admit) the coming of Jesus Christ (the Messiah) in bodily form. Such a one is the imposter (the seducer, the deceiver, the false leader, the antagonist of Christ) and the antichrist.

2 JOHN 1:7 (AMP)

The Rapture

Christ returns to this world in glory, we'll not all sleep but will change this encourage us to live on call be ready at any time in a flash and twinkling of an eye the archangel trumpet call of God. Dead believer's proceeds live ones and won't miss God sees to them accompanying his return Christians who died will unto as human and divine being in Christ. Christians alive remember in mind through higher calling. Rapture strong feeling absorbing your mind with great joy in the spirit.

BY: MARY M. JOHNSON

And so return unto thee with all their heart, and with all their soul, in the land if their soul, in the land of their enemies, which led them away captive, and pray unto thee toward their land, which thou hast chosen, and the house which I have built for thy name:

2 KING 8:48 (KJV)

If they repent and turn to You with all their mind and with all their heart in the land of their enemies who tool them captive, and pray to You toward their land which You gave to their fathers, the city which You have chose, and the house which I have built for Your Name

2 KING 8:48 (AMP)

The Heavenly Wedding

The lamb and his wife has come she made
Herself ready for the heavenly
Boundaries she's glittering in
White and pure linen taking
Her over the threshold of truth
And righteousness.
Making her happy and full of
Mirth he adores this city of
His love ones, beautiful trees,
Snowflakes, roses the streets
Are pave with gold and the
Gates are pearl.
No lies and corruption of life
Won't manifest no separation
Between his people sinners
Thrown in the lake of fire and
Brimstone. We are all and all
In one, he takes care of is
People.
The throne of God and the lamb in the midst, they shall serve him.

BY: MARY M. JOHNSON

The next day Jon seeth Jesus coming unto him, and saith, Behold the Lamb of God, which taketh away the sin of the world.

JOHN 1:29 (KJV)

The Next say John saw Jesus coming to him and said, Look! There is the Lamb of God, Who takes away the sin of the world!

2 KING 8:48 (AMP)

Meaning for my words:

Poetic: possessing the qualities or charm of poetry: poetic descriptions of nature.

My heart is inditing a good matter: I speak of the things which I have made touching the king: my tongue [is] the pen a skillful poet.

PSA 45:1 (NLT)

Journey: passage or progress from one stage to another: the journey to *success*.

And the LORD said unto me, Arise, take [thy] journey before the people, that they may go in and possess the land, which I swear unto their fathers to give unto them.

DEU. 10:11 (KJV)

Of An

Joyous: having a happy nature or mood; joyful

Come, let us sing to the LORD! Let us give a joyous shout to the rock of our salvation!

PSA 95:1(NLT)

Outcome: a final product or end result; consequence; issue.

Remember those who rule over you, who have spoken the word of God to you, whose faith follow, considering the **outcome** of their conduct.

HBR 13:7 (NKJV)

Poetic Journey of an Joyous Outcome

The Journey of life is an adventure.

MRS. MARY M. JOHNSON

His words are Poetic instructions for your life. Taken the journey with God you will not make a mistake. You will encounter higher and greater designations for whom you are and what you are able to do though him. His words are like a river of flowing water if you drink from the brook then you will get full.

Take fast hold of instruction; let her not go; keep her; for she is thy life. Proverbs 4:13

Take firm hold of instructions, do not let go; guard her; for she is your life.
Proverbs 4:13 (amp)

I HAVE WRITTEN THESE POEMS TO ENLIGHTEN YOU HEART AND YOUR SPIRITUAL MIND. I HOPE YOU WILL ENJOY READING THEM AS MUCH AS I ENJOYED GOD GIVEN THEM TO ME.

MAY GOD BLESS YOU!